UNITED STATES NAV

SOUTH DAKOTA CLASS BATTLESHIPS

by Steve Wiper

USS SOUTH DAKOTA BB-57, Puget Sound Naval Shipyard, 24 August 1944.

CLASSIC WARSHIPS PUBLISHING

P. O. Box 57591 • Tucson, AZ. 85732 • USA
Web Site: www.classicwarships.com • Ph/Fx (520)748-2992
Copyright © September 2009
ISBN 978-0-9823583-1-3
Printed by Arizona Lithographers, Tucson, Arizona

GENERAL HISTORY OF THE SOUTH DAKOTA CLASS BATTLESHIPS

The design of the SOUTH DAKOTA class battleships grew out of the intention of the US Navy to build an additional two NORTH CAROLINA class battleships. Discussions began in 1936, but by 1937, the Chief of Naval Operations insisted on a new design, which delayed construction until US Congress authorized the program into the 1939 budget.

In order for the US Navy design of this new class of battleship to remain within the 1921 Washington Naval Treaty limit, and have better armor protection than the previous NORTH CAROLINA class, a complete re-design was necessary. The hull would be shorter, but remain at the same maximum width, not just for stability when firing the main battery, but also because of the limit of 108 ft., due to the width of the Panama Canal. The increase in armor protection necessitated placement of the side armor belt to be inboard, resulting in cramped hull compartments and a reduction in underwater protection.

As other nations were building faster battleships, this new class would need to attain a top speed of 27 knots. To do this, the design required greater shaft power than the previous design. A shaft horse power of 130,000 was attained, resulting in a top speed of 27.5 kts.

The armament for this new class of American battleship was a repeat of the previous NORTH CAROLINA class, with three triple 16 in./45 cal. main armament turrets, and ten twin 5 in./38 cal. dual purpose (DP) secondary mounts. A minor exception to the SOUTH DAKOTA, in that she was fitted with eight twin 5 in. DP mounts. This was because she was constructed with a larger conning tower and expanded accommodations for flag-ship capabilities. The medium and light anti-aircraft (AA) weaponry was also a repeat of the previous class, as well as the catapult arrangement and observation aircraft carried.

U.S.S. ALABAMA (BB60)
BOW VIEW ON BLDG. WAYS
NORFOLK NAVY YARD PORTSMOUTH, VA.
PHOTO SERIAL 10-62-29 DEC. 30, 1940

Even though the following IOWA class battleships, a newer and much better design, was completing it's design at the same time, as well as being ordered for construction to begin in 1940, the authorization of the SOUTH DAKOTA class was ordered, with construction beginning in 1939. SOUTH DAKOTA (BB-57) was laid down 5 July 1939 at New York Shipbuilding, INDIANA (BB-58) on 20 November 1939 at Newport News Shipbuilding, MASSACHUSETTS (BB-59) 20 July 1939 at Bethlehem Shipbuilding, Quincy, and ALABAMA (BB-60) 1 February 1940 at the Norfolk Navy Yard.

The photograph to the left is of the BB-60 ALABAMA under construction at the Norfolk Navy Yard, 1 November 1940. The photograph below is of BB-57 SOUTH DAKOTA, launched 7 June 1941 at the New York Shipbuilding Yard.

SOUTH DAKOTA was the first of these new battleships to be launched on 7 June 1941, followed by the MASSACHUSETTS on 23 September 1941. Soon after, the INDIANA was launched on 21 November 1941, which was followed a few months later by the ALABAMA on 16 February 1942.

After launching, the fitting-out phase of construction was to follow. This consisted of the build-up of the superstructure, installation of the main, secondary and anti-aircraft armaments, deck fittings, aircraft handling equipment and an incredible number of other items necessary to complete each battleship prior to their commissioning into the US Navy. It would be at that point that each warship commissioned into the USN would then receive the prefix USS, which stood for United States Ship.

MASSACHUSETTS *during her fitting out phase of construction, taken at the Bethlehem shipyard in Quincy Massachusetts, 8 October 1941. The other vessels also fitting out are, left to right, the fast oiler Sinclair Superflame,* ATLANTA *class light cruisers* SAN DIEGO *and* SAN JUAN.

BB 59 U. S. S. MASSACHUSETTS
HULL 1478
SINCLAIR SUPERFLAME HULL 1490
CL 53 U. S. S. SAN DIEGO HULL 1479
CL 54 U. S. S. SAN JUAN HULL 1480
VIEW AT OUTFITTING DOCK
BETH. STEEL CO. SHIPBLDG. DIV.
QUINCY, MASS. OCT. 8, 1941

H-378- M 64
U.S.S. INDIANA (BB 58)
LOOKING AFT
N.N.S. & D.D.Co.
DATE: 11-1-41

4

The image to the left is of INDIANA completing construction prior to launching, 1 November 1941. This image is of INDIANA fitting out in one of the dry docks at the Newport News shipyard, 9 March 1942.

NO. 78
INDIANA (BB58)
DRY DOCK - LOOKING FORWARD
S + D.D.CO.
E: 3-9-42.

OFFICIAL PHOTOGRAPH
NOT TO BE RELEASED
FOR PUBLICATION

U.S.S. ALABAMA (BB60)
STERN VIEW AT FITTING OUT BERTH
NORFOLK NAVY YARD   PORTSMOUTH, VA.
PHOTO SERIAL 10-172-48   JULY 3, 1942

U.S.S. ALABAMA (BB60)
BOW VIEW AT FITTING OUT BERTH
NORFOLK NAVY YARD   PORTSMOUTH, VA.
PHOTO SERIAL 10-174-50   JULY 3, 1942

The USS SOUTH DAKOTA BB-58 was commissioned into the US Navy on 20 March 1942. At that time, she was not completed and was moved to the Philadelphia Navy Yard to finish fitting out. This task was completed by the end of May and she began her shakedown period and crew training during the months of June and July of 1942, based out of the Philadelphia Navy Yard. This took place in the Atlantic Ocean.

USS INDIANA BB-58 was commissioned on 30 April 1942 at the Newport News shipyard. After completion of construction by the end of July, she would perform her shakedown cruises and crew training during the months of August and September of 1942. She also performed this in the Atlantic Ocean and in Casco Bay, off of Portland, Maine.

USS Indiana, the 35,000 ton battlewagon as she lay at her berth in Newport News, Va., on the day of her commissioning, April 30, 1942.

U. S. GOVERNMENT PRINTING OFFICE 16—1

The USS MASSACHUSETTS BB-59 was commissioned on 12 May 1942 at the Boston Navy Yard. She completed fitting out by the end of July. She would perform her shakedown cruises and crew training during the months of August through mid October, sometimes in company with BB-58. This took place in the Atlantic Ocean and at Casco Bay, Maine.

By this time the USS SOUTH DAKOTA was en route to the Pacific, via the Panama Canal, passing through on 21 August 1942. She arrived at the Tonga Islands, via Pearl Harbor, on 4 September, but two days later, struck an unchartered reef, badly damaging her bow. BB-57 was forced to return to Pearl Harbor for dry docking and repairs, arriving there in Mid-September.

In the meantime, USS ALABAMA BB-60 was commissioned on 16 August 1942 at the Norfolk Navy Yard. After fitting out was completed in early November, she commenced her shakedown cruises and crew training in the Chesapeake Bay, moving to the Atlantic and later to Casco Bay. This continued thru early January 1943.

Another view of BB-58 on commissioning day, 30 April 1942.

USS MASSACHUSETTS BB-59 *in Boston Harbor, 12 May 1942, the day of her commissioning. She was not completed at that time. Items such as radar antenna, and the medium and some of the light anti-aircraft weaponry have yet to be installed. BB-59 was painted in a Measure 12 Revised camouflage pattern at that time.*

The photos on these pages are [of] USS SOUTH DAKOTA [BB]-57, after commissioning, [du]ring her shake down period, [ab]out June 1942. Compare her [lay]out of twin 5in. 38cal. sec-[on]dary mounts to that of her [si]sterships. BB-57 was painted [at] that time in a Measure 12 [Re]vised (Ms. 12R) camouflage [pa]ttern consisting of Navy [Bl]ue (5-N), Ocean Gray (5-O) [an]d Haze Gray (5-H) on her [ver]tical surfaces and Deck Blue [(2]0-B) on all horizontal sur-[fa]ces.

SOUTH DAKOTA carried three Vought OS2U Kingfisher floatplanes for observation and scouting purposes at the time of this photograph. She was in Battleship Division 6 (BatDiv 6), so the fuselage numbering of 6-O-7 thru 6-O-9 tell us that BB-57 was the third vessel of BatDiv 6. The "6" was for the BatDiv, while the "O" stood for battleships and the numbers "7" thru "9" were the aircraft designator. Each battleship carried three aircraft. USS WASHINGTON BB-56 and NORTH CAROLINA BB-55 were the other two battleships in that division at that time.

USS MASSACHUSETTS BB-59 *during her trial period, painted in a Ms. 12 Revised camouflage pattern, dated 13 July 1942. Note the painting of the main gun barrels. The paint colors were Navy Blue (5-N), Ocean Gray (5-O) and Haze Gray (5-H) on the vertical surfaces and Deck Blue (20-B) on all decks and horizontal surfaces. The general rule of Ms. 12 Revised camouflage was for 5-N and 5-O to painted on the hull and 5-O and 5-H to be painted on the superstructure, but there were exceptions to that rule, as in this case. BB-59 had a patch of 5-H on the bow, and in some areas, the continuation of 5-N, up into the superstructure.*

At this time, BB-59 was equipped with a Mk. 3 fire control radar, the antenna mounted atop both her fore and aft Mk. 38 main battery directors. All four secondary battery Mk. 37 directors were equipped with Mk. 4 fire control radar, with their antenna mounted atop those directors. For air search radar, she was fitted with SC radar, with the antenna mounted atop the foremast. Her surface search radar was SG, it's antenna mounted at the leading edge of the forward fire control platform, with a visibility of 270°, looking forward and to the sides, but not aft.

USS INDIANA BB-58 *during her shakedown period, during May 1942. She was painted is one of the more diverse patterns of Ms. 12 Revised. The colors were the standard Navy Blue, Ocean Gray and Haze Gray, but the pattern was much more liberal in it's application. In fact, if one were to study camouflage patterns of the British Royal Navy of the time, there is some similarity, almost a merging of the two systems. With the Ms. 12 Revised, no deck pattern was applied. All decks, horizontal and semi horizontal surfaces were painted with Deck Blue.*

The radar fitted to INDIANA at this time was not complete. Missing are the main battery fire control and the surface search radar antenna. The secondary fire control Mk. 37 directors did have their Mk. 4 radar antenna fitted. Also, the SC air search radar antenna was fitted atop the foremast.

Note the subtle differences in the construction of various platforms on and around the bridge tower from ship to ship within the SOUTH DAKOTA class battleships.

All three vertical surface paint colors in BB-58's camouflage pattern were applied to both the hull and the superstructure. In this photograph, dated 8 September 1942, the latest in main battery fire control radar systems has been installed. Only on the forward Mk. 38 director, a Mk. 8 FC radar antenna is visible. Also, the SG surface search radar antenna is visible on the leading edge of the fire control platform atop the bridge.

On both this page and the previous are photos of BB-58 at anchor in Hampton Roads, Virginia, during the period of July thru September 1942. She was conducting crew familiarization and training, as well as calibrating her machinery and weapon systems. This was conducted at port, in the Atlantic Ocean, as well as in Casco Bay, Maine. The image below is a rare port side view of USS INDIANA in her unique Ms. 12R camouflage pattern.

USS SOUTH DAKOTA *with escorting destroyers in the background, during the opening phase of the "Battle of Santa Cruz," 26 October 1942. The image below is also of BB-57 running at high speed and putting up a wall of anti-aircraft fire in an effort to shot down attacking Japanese carrier bourn aircraft.*

SOUTH DAKOTA *and* ENTERPRISE *maneuvering in an attempt to evade attacking Japanese carrier aircraft. In this photograph,* ENTERPRISE *is near-missed by a bomb while an Aichi D3A1 "Val" dive bomber is about to crash into the sea.*

USS SOUTH DAKOTA completed repairs at Pearl Harbor by early October 1942. She also received an additional four quad 40mm AA mounts, replacing two quad 1.1in. AA mounts, giving her a mixed battery of medium AA. She also received twenty 20mm single AA mounts.

She began training with Task Force 16 (TF16), built around the fleet aircraft carrier USS ENTERPRISE CV-6. They departed Pearl Harbor 16 October and headed for the Solomon Islands, joined by TF17, built around USS HORNET CV-8, off of Espiritu Santo, south of the Solomon and Santa Cruz Islands.

On 26 October 1942, Japanese carrier aircraft attacked the HORNET group and within one hour, attacked the ENTERPRISE group. Their focus was upon CV-6, enabling BB-57 to put up a highly effective AA defense. The enemy aircraft turned their attack also upon BB-57. Only one hit was scored and one near miss. A short time later 14 torpedo bombers attacked, all missing. In less than an hour, 29 dive bombers attacked, scoring only one hit atop turret #1. The hit caused only minor damage to the turret roof, but severe damage to two gun barrels on turret #2, rendering both guns inoperable. One man was killed and 50 wounded. SOUTH DAKOTA claimed an incredible 26 aircraft shot down, but later examination of gun mount reports show multiple mounts claiming the same kill. It would appear that the number of Japanese aircraft shot down was somewhere between 11 and 20, still an excellent kill record, one that still stands to this day. USS HORNET was sunk during this battle.

A Nakajima B5N2 "Kate" torpedo bomber flying between US Navy warships during an attack upon SOUTH DAKOTA. *Two aircraft were attacking, one shot down prior to the taking of this photo and this aircraft flew over BB-57's stern and crashed into the sea. Both torpedoes missed their intended target.*

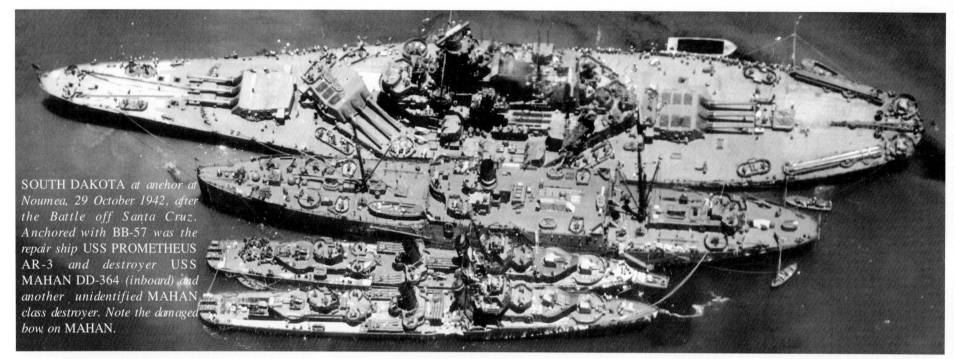

SOUTH DAKOTA *at anchor at Noumea, 29 October 1942, after the Battle off Santa Cruz. Anchored with BB-57 was the repair ship* USS PROMETHEUS AR-3 *and destroyer* USS MAHAN DD-364 *(inboard) and another unidentified* MAHAN *class destroyer. Note the damaged bow on* MAHAN.

While departing the Santa Cruz Islands, SOUTH DAKOTA collided with the destroyer USS MAHAN DD-364 while maneuvering to avoid a submarine contact. BB-57 received damage to five of her outboard fuel oil tanks, while DD-364 had her bow crushed. The fleet arrived at Noumea, New Caledonia and both vessels were repaired for collision and battle damage.

On 11 November, her damage repaired, except for the two gun barrels on turret #2, SOUTH DAKOTA, with TF16 departed Noumea and sortied for the Guadalcanal area. During the dates of 12 to 15 November 1942, the IJN attempted a large scale sustained assault upon Guadalcanal.

The First Naval Battle of Guadalcanal took place south, off the island of Savo, just offshore of Guadalcanal in the early morning hours, Friday, 13 November, beginning at 0150hrs. This melee between USN and IJN warships was so chaotic, as the warships mixed together, firing upon one another, only for ten minutes, that it became known by the Americans as a "Bar Room Brawl." When dawn came, the IJN and the USN had lost several warships each and several others each, were adrift in the area, severely damaged. The survivors from both Navy's licked their wounds and limped home during that day, as well as the next.

During the night of 13 November, the IJN was able to bombard Henderson Field on Guadalcanal with heavy cruisers. They were able to retire from the area unscathed in the early hours of 14 November, but were later hit hard by aircraft from ENTERPRISE, sinking one heavy cruiser and severely damaging two others.

On the night of 14-15 November, the Second Naval Battle of Guadalcanal took place, beginning about 2317hrs., when USN battleships opened fire upon an IJN light cruiser and destroyer. The USN force, TF 64, consisted of the battleships WASHINGTON and SOUTH DAKOTA and four destroyers, while the IJN force consisted of the battleship KIRISHIMA, two heavy cruisers, two light cruisers and eleven destroyers. The two forces made contact off of Guadalcanal, southeast of Savo Island.

The two USN battleships ceased fire with no results at 2322hrs., but USN destroyers opened fire upon IJN destroyers at 2325hrs., at which time the IJN destroyers returned fire.

At 2333hrs., SOUTH DAKOTA suddenly lost all electrical power throughout the entire battleship. Her gunfire caused circuits to overload and because those circuits were locked down, the entire electrical system shorted out. The battleship was then blacked out, but still able to steer manually. She was unable to operate all but her light AA mounts, which were useless in a night ship-to-ship gun engagement.

By 2335hrs., SOUTH DAKOTA steered to starboard to avoid the USS PRESTON DD-379 which was on fire just ahead. WASHINGTON stayed straight on course, as the two battleships separated. At 2336hrs., PRESTON was hit by a torpedo and sank. 2338hrs., SOUTH DAKOTA started to regain power to portions of the ship, but was still experiencing significant random power losses. Another USN destroyer, USS WALKE DD-416, was hit by a torpedo, blowing off her bow all the way back to her bridge, sinking soon after. The third USN destroyer, USS BENHAM DD-397 also took a torpedo in the bow at that time. The fourth USN destroyer, USS GWIN DD-433 was hit badly by IJN destroyer gunfire and turned away, with BENHAM and retired to the west, out of the fight. That left WASHINGTON as the remaining USN combatant without damage. It was also about this time that the destroyer HIJMS AYANAMI sank from damage by USN destroyer gunfire.

About 2341hrs., SOUTH DAKOTA had electrical fires breaking out in several locations internally. Soon thereafter, she fired her after turret at targets astern, igniting her own OS2U observation aircraft, the fires illuminating the aft end of BB-57. The following salvo then blew the aircraft right off the stern of the battleship.

The Japanese force illuminated SOUTH DAKOTA with searchlights about 2348hrs. The majority of the IJN force then concentrated their fire upon SOUTH DAKOTA. Over the next sixteen minutes, beginning at 2349hrs., and ending at 0005hrs., she was hit by at least 27 enemy shells, mostly in the area of the superstructure. In the meantime, WASHINGTON ranged in on KIRISHIMA during this time. She opened fire at 0000hrs., and ceased fire at 0007hrs., firing 75 main battery rounds and achieving at least 9 hits and possibly as many as 20. KIRISHIMA also received numerous 5in. hits. She turned away burning heavily and came to a stop, all systems inoperable.

By 0015hrs., SOUTH DAKOTA began to exit the battle area,

This photo of the bridge tower on BB-57 shows the shell damage from the night engagement during the Second Naval Battle of Guadalcanal. During that engagement with the Imperial Japanese Navy, SOUTH DAKOTA, illuminated by searchlights, received the concentrated fire of the IJN bombardment force of destroyers, light and heavy cruisers and the battleship HIJMS KIRISHIMA. She was hit by at least 27 enemy shells of various calibers from 5in., 5.5in., 6in., 8in. and at least one 14in.

F644C3432   NAVY YARD, NEW YORK   NOVEMBER 1942
U.S.S. BB 57   PHOTO #54   TAKEN BY SHIP
OUTSIDE VIEW LOOKG. AFT OF HOLES IN WIND & SPRAY SHIELD FWD. FR.
79 CL SKY LOOKOUT STATION.

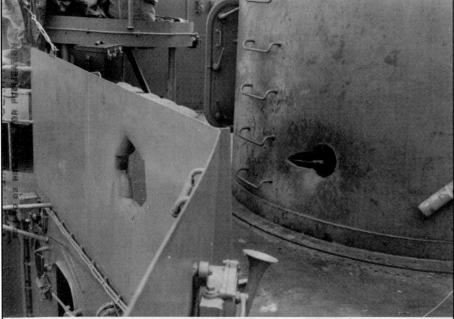

The photographs on this page are of the damage that SOUTH DAKOTA received during the night engagement of the Second Naval Battle of Guadalcanal. These images were part of the "Battle Damage Report" that the US Navy would together to help analyze what damage was incurred and how to counter such damage in the future. It was also used to analyze the effectiveness of the enemy's armament. The two images to the left show the effect of a shell that passed right through the superstructure and luckily did not explode. It still did significant damage to the battleship.

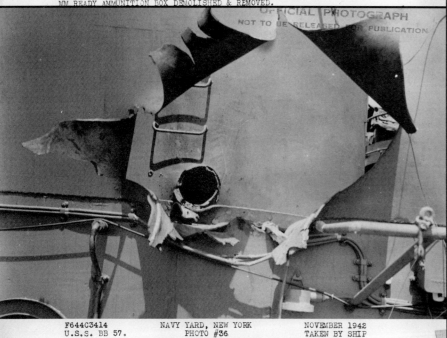

fighting many fires and trying to regain operation of her radar and communication systems, as she slowly steamed south and to the west of Guadalcanal. During this time WASHINGTON turned north, west of Savo Island to continue the fight with the IJN and to draw them away from the retiring BB-57 and the two remaining destroyers. By 0033hrs., BB-56 turned to the south, pursued by several IJN destroyers and a light cruiser, but she managed to outrun them.

In the meantime KIRISHIMA was in a bad way. She had lost all power and steering and was badly afire. There were many casualties and the battleship was listing heavily. Efforts by other IJN warships to assist her were in vain, unable to stop the progressive flooding,

she capsized and sank about 5 miles west of Savo Island at 0223hrs.

SOUTH DAKOTA meet BB-56 and the two damaged destroyers south of Guadalcanal at a pre-arranged point and the crippled fleet steamed to Noumea, New Caledonia for repairs. BB-57 received major damage to her superstructure during the battle, with 38 killed and 60 wounded, but she was lucky, as it could have been much worse. WASHINGTON's attack upon KIRISHIMA saved SOUTH DAKOTA. BB-57 headed for the US east coast for major repairs, via the Panama Canal, arriving at New York Navy Yard, 8 December 1942.

USS MASSACHUSETTS BB-59

steamed from Casco Bay, Maine and joined TF 34, as flagship, 24 October 1942. They headed for Casablanca, Morocco, via Gibraltar, arriving there in the night of 7 November. This was Operation Torch, the Allied invasion of French Morocco, with BB-59 leading the largest naval fleet ever assembled to that date.

The invasion began at 0630hrs., 8 November 1942, when French shore batteries fired upon the invasion and support vessels as they approached the beach to land. BB-59 was in formation 10 miles offshore of Casablanca Harbor with the heavy cruisers USS WICHITA CA-45 and the TUSCALOOSA CA-44. By 0700hrs., one of BB-59's OS2Us was returning with French fighters in pursuit, the USN warships shotting down one fighter, with the other

BB-59, *en route to the North African Coast, lost a OS2U Kingfisher observation aircraft to storm damage in the Atlantic Ocean, 4 November 1942, during that crossing.*

aircraft turning back. Then, French shore batteries shifted fire onto BB-59 and the cruisers. Also at this time, the new and incomplete French battleship JEAN BART, tied up at a pier in Casablanca Harbor, opened fire with her one operating 15in. four gun turret upon BB-59 and the cruisers out to sea.

It was at 0704hrs. that MASSACHUSETTS opened fire upon JEAN BART. She ceased fire at 0833hrs. BB-59 had numerous problems with the shock from firing her main guns temporarily knocking out all radar systems. Fire from JEAN BART was ineffective, with no hits on the USN warships. JEAN BART was hit by BB-59 five times with extensive damage, as well as sinking a destroyer tied up astern. Extensive shell damage was also done to port facilities by the USN warships.

During the later portion of this bombardment, seven French destroyers sortied from Casablanca Harbor to attack the landing force 13 miles to the east, guarded only be the cruisers USS AUGUSTA CA-31, USS BROOKLYN CL-40 and destroyers. At 0855hrs., MASSACHUSETTS and her cruisers headed at top speed to intercept those French destroyers. The French destroyers were engaged about 0918hrs. by the USN cruisers and BB-59. USN cruisers continued east, but BB-59 turned back west to avoid a destroyer torpedo attack. She was capable of ranging in on the French destroyers from much further away than the USN cruisers.

During this time, MASSACHUSETTS again experienced radar systems failures from the shock of firing her own main guns. About 1000hrs., TUSCALOOSA and BB-59 hit and sank a French destroyer, but BB-59 came under fire from shore batteries, hit once by an 7.6in shell with minor damage. At 1005hrs., BB-59 then came under torpedo attack from an unknown French submarine. She managed to evade them, one narrowly missed by less than 15ft. Also at this time a French light cruiser and two additional destroyers sortied from Casablanca towards the invasion force to the east. These were engaged by the USN cruisers and kept at bay.

MASSACHUSETTS resumed fire upon Casablanca Harbor targets at 1035hrs. Again at 1100hrs., she shifted fire back to the French destroyers that were engaged by USN cruisers, helping to sink another and drive off the French light cruiser with heavy damage. During that time she was hit by a 5.1in round that inflicted little damage.

There was a lull in fighting until that afternoon when USN warships, including BB-59 engaged minor French Navy vessels and the shore batteries around Casablanca. BB-59 ceased fire at 1355hrs. to conserve ammunition in case the French battleship RICHELIEU sortied from Dakar to oppose the Allied invasion force. This never materialized and the naval engagement ended with BB-59 "clearing her guns" with one last salvo at the shore batteries. MASSACHUSETTS expended just over 60% of her main battery ammunition, her 16in. guns fired 786 shells and her 5in. secondary mounts fired 221 rounds.

On 12 November 1942, BB-59 departed the North African Coast for the United States, arriving at the Norfolk Navy Yard, 22 November 1942. She would soon steam to the Boston Navy Yard for a major refit, later gunnery practice off Portland, Maine, in Casco Bay, into February 1943.

On the stern, looking forward upon the after turret and superstructure of USS MASSACHUSETTS BB-59 during a lull in the naval engagement off the French port of Casablanca, Morocco. Note the 20mm single AA mount without the normal protective mount tub to the left side of this photo. The writing on the inside of it's gun shield reads "Lead Damnit Lead," to make gunners take proper aim at their aircraft targets. The radar antenna fitted atop the Mk. 38 main battery directors is for her Mk. 3 fire control radar. Those fitted atop the smaller Mk. 37 secondary directors was for the Mk. 4 fire control radar system. An SC air search antenna was mounted atop the foremast. Note that the after deck in the aircraft handling area is steel, as that was wood covered in both the NORTH CAROLINA and IOWA class battleships.

USS ALABAMA BB-60 *at anchor, during her shakedown period, in Lynn Haven Roads, off of Virginia Beach, Virginia. She was painted in a Ms. 12R camouflage pattern in the standard colors of 5-N, 5-O and 5-H. Careful study of the photos on this and the following page show her pattern to be somewhat irregular. This photo was taken 1 December 1942.*

Below is an aerial image of BB-60 *underway in Hampton Roads, 1 December 1942.*

USS ALABAMA BB-60 *in Hampton Roads, off of the Norfolk Navy Yard, Norfolk, Virginia, 1 December 1942. The irregularities about this camouflage pattern applied to BB-60 are the use of the lightest color, 5-H running from the superstructure down, onto the hull. Also the use of 5-N from the hull, up into the superstructure.*

USS INDIANA BB-58 *at anchor off of Noumea, New Caledonia. These photos were taken from* USS SARATOGA CV-3, *17 December 1942. BB-58 was then painted in a Ms. 22 camouflage pattern, the paint colors consisting of 5-N on the hull and 5-H on every vertical surface above 5-N. The decks and horizontal surfaces were painted with 20-B. Note the Mk. 8 FC radar antenna atop the Mk. 38 main battery directors. This was a much improved system over the earlier Mk. 3 radar. At that time she was still fitted with the SC air search radar, the antenna mounted on her foremast.*

Below are two images of SOUTH DAKOTA taken at the conclusion of her refit to repair battle damage incurred at the Second Naval Battle of Guadalcanal.

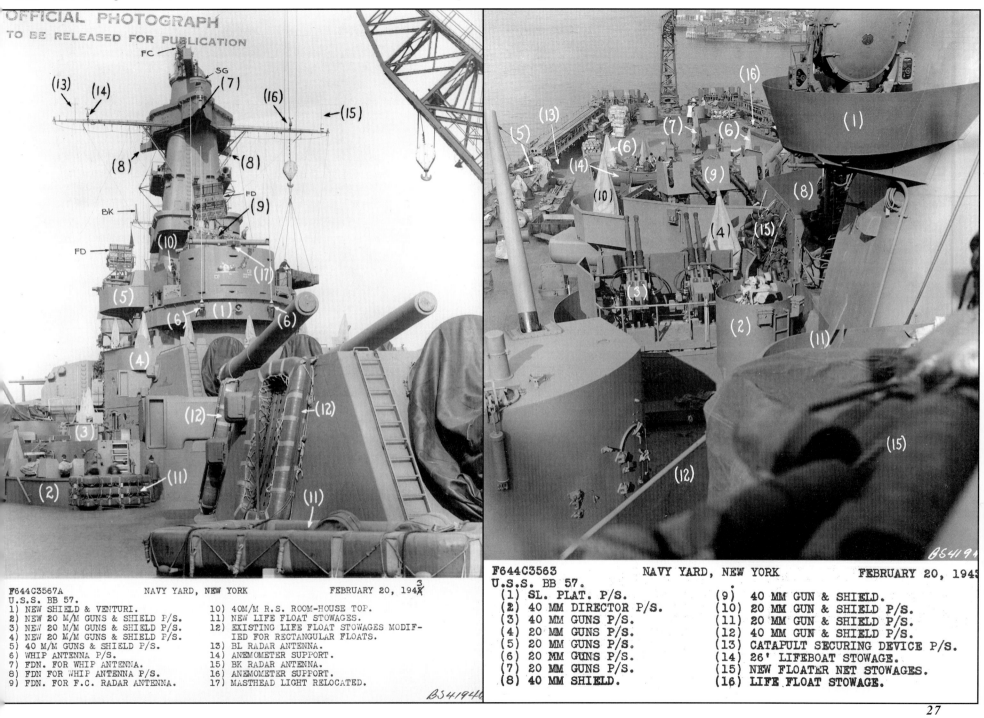

F644C3567A   NAVY YARD, NEW YORK   FEBRUARY 20, 1943
U.S.S. BB 57.
1) NEW SHIELD & VENTURI.
2) NEW 20 M/M GUNS & SHIELD P/S.
3) NEW 20 M/M GUNS & SHIELD P/S.
4) NEW 20 M/M GUNS & SHIELD P/S.
5) 40 M/M GUNS & SHIELD P/S.
6) WHIP ANTENNA P/S.
7) FDN. FOR WHIP ANTENNA.
8) FDN FOR WHIP ANTENNA P/S.
9) FDN. FOR F.C. RADAR ANTENNA.
10) 40M/M R.S. ROOM-HOUSE TOP.
11) NEW LIFE FLOAT STOWAGES.
12) EXISTING LIFE FLOAT STOWAGES MODIF-
     IED FOR RECTANGULAR FLOATS.
13) BL RADAR ANTENNA.
14) ANEMOMETER SUPPORT.
15) BK RADAR ANTENNA.
16) ANEMOMETER SUPPORT.
17) MASTHEAD LIGHT RELOCATED.

BS41940

F644C3563   NAVY YARD, NEW YORK   FEBRUARY 20, 1943
U.S.S. BB 57.
(1) SL. PLAT. P/S.
(2) 40 MM DIRECTOR P/S.
(3) 40 MM GUNS P/S.
(4) 20 MM GUNS P/S.
(5) 20 MM GUNS P/S.
(6) 20 MM GUNS P/S.
(7) 20 MM GUNS P/S.
(8) 40 MM SHIELD.
(9) 40 MM GUN & SHIELD.
(10) 20 MM GUN & SHIELD P/S.
(11) 20 MM GUN & SHIELD P/S.
(12) 40 MM GUN & SHIELD P/S.
(13) CATAPULT SECURING DEVICE P/S.
(14) 26' LIFEBOAT STOWAGE.
(15) NEW FLOATER NET STOWAGES.
(16) LIFE FLOAT STOWAGE.

BS41941

BB-57 *at the conclusion of her refit at the New York Navy Yard. This photo was taken 23 February 1943. Note that* SOUTH DAKOTA *was then painted in a Ms. 21 camouflage of 5-N, an overall Navy Blue, with decks and horizontal surfaces painted in Deck Blue 20-B. Also note that only the after Mk. 38 main battery director was fitted with a upgraded Mk. 8 FC radar.*

USS INDIANA BB-58 began combat operations on 9 November 1942 when she arrived at Pearl Harbor and later steamed for Noumea, New Caledonia. She joined with USS NORTH CAROLINA BB-55, and WASHINGTON, replacing SOUTH DAKOTA, at Noumea, 28 November. They would operate as a distant covering force to the aircraft carriers ENTERPRISE and SARATOGA. BB-58 also covered troop and invasion convoys in the Solomon Island campaign for the following few months, into early 1943. In this role she acted as an AA escort and performed bombardment duties for landings. This time was rather uneventful for INDIANA.

ALABAMA returned to the US east coast and continued training in Chesapeake Bay through January and into February 1943. She joined Task Group 22 (TG 22) and returned to Casco Bay for tactical maneuvers and battle practice with SOUTH DAKOTA in March, who had just finished her battle damage refit. BB-58 also performed maneuvers with BB-57 and the aircraft carrier USS RANGER CV-4 in the North Atlantic during the later part of March, into April 1943. During this time the two battleships operated with the RANGER to protect convoys in the North Atlantic Ocean en route to Murmansk, Russia. SOUTH DAKOTA and ALABAMA were the long range escort for

those convoys in the event that the German battleships SCHARNHORST and TIRPITZ, or the heavy cruiser LÜTZOW sortied to attack the Murmansk bound convoys.

In the meantime, MASSACHUSETTS departed the US east coast in late February 1943 and transited the Panama Canal en route to Pearl Harbor. From there she departed for Noumea, New Caledonia, arriving there 4 March 1943. She joined her sistership INDIANA and battleship WASHINGTON, replacing NORTH CAROLINA who departed to Pearl Harbor for a refit and upgrade. The battleships bombarded Russell Island in that invasion during April 1943.

USS ALABAMA BB-60 *during her shakedown cruise and crew training in the North Atlantic Ocean and in Casco Bay, off of Portland Maine, during December 1942, into January 1943. Many of the color photos of BB-60 that were taken during this time show the effects of extreme cold in their discoloration of the image.*

Above, USS ALABAMA BB-60 *at sea in high winds, 4 March 1943, off of the US East Coast.*

BB-60 *from* USS RANGER CV-4, *28 March 1943, possibly in Casco Bay, Maine. She was painted into a Ms. 22 camouflage on her last yard period, more than likely sometime in February 1943.*

ALABAMA and SOUTH DAKOTA began operations with the British Royal Navy, Home Fleet, during mid-April, based out of Argentia, Newfoundland. They would later be based out of Scapa Flow, beginning in mid-May 1943. This was done to reinforce the Royal Navy (RN) in the North Atlantic due to their efforts to build their strength in the Mediterranean theater of operations. The British appeal for assistance was answered with the assignment of these two battleships and an escort of five destroyers. BB-57 and BB-60 worked with heavy units of the RN through July 1943. Their duty included long range escort of Murmansk bound convoys. They operated with the RN battleships KING GEORGE V, DUKE OF YORK and ANSON.

Early in June 1943, both SOUTH DAKOTA and ALABAMA, along with RN Home Fleet units, covered the reinforcement of the garrison on the island of Spitzbergen. This was an important North Atlantic weather station manned by Allied Forces. It is located between the Barents Sea and the Arctic Ocean, over 1000 miles north of the Arctic Circle. This was possibly the furthest north that any American battleship has ever ventured.

Later in July 1943, both American bat-tleships participated, with RN Home Fleet heavy units in "Operation Governor," a diversion aimed toward southern Norway, to draw German attention away from Allied operations in the invasion of Sicily, Italy. It had also been devised to attempt to lure out the German battleships and heavy cruisers into battle. This was unsuccessful, with the German heavy units remaining in their Norwegian fjord anchorages.

On 1 August 1943, both SOUTH DAKOTA and ALABAMA and their screening destroyers, detached from the RN Home Fleet and steamed for the Norfolk Navy Yard. This TF arrived at Norfolk on 9 August 1943.

Another view, a close-up of the superstructure of ALABAMA, *this photograph taken from CV-4, sometime during March 1943. She was painted in Ms. 22 camouflage at the time of this photo. She also has the upgraded Mk. 8 FC radar, the antenna visible atop the Mk. 38 main battery directors. It appears that she still retained the SC air search radar, the antenna mounted atop the foremast.*

This historic color photograph of the stern of ALABAMA is a great view of many details on this area of the battleship. The large boom projecting out from the starboard of her hull was known as a "Boat Boom," to which the ships boats could be kept in the water at ready and were tied up to this boom. The aircraft on the starboard catapult was a Vought OS2U Kingfisher observation floatplane. The SOUTH DAKOTA class battleships carried three such aircraft. This image was taken sometime in 1943.

Another great historic color photo taken aboard BB-60, sometime in late 1942, or early 1943. She was operating in Casco Bay, Maine, or out in the North Atlantic Ocean in the vicinity of Newfoundland. During that time she was going through her shakedown cruise and crew training.

SOUTH DAKOTA *in Scapa Flow, Great Britain, during June 1943, while operating with the Royal Navy Home Fleet. She was undertaking anti-aircraft firing practice and maneuvering at the time this photograph was taken. The aircraft in this image is a Beaufighter.*

From the stern deck of the HMS KING GEORGE V, the American battleships SOUTH DAKOTA and ALABAMA, during a voyage with the British Royal Navy Home Fleet. The date of this photograph is believed to be sometime during July 1943. Note the differences in the camouflage painting of the two American battleships. BB-57 was painted in Ms. 21 and BB-60 was painted in Ms. 22. Ms. 21 was possibly a better camouflage application for night engagements.

All four images on this and the preceding page are historic photographs of USS ALABAMA BB-60 in early December 1942, during her shakedown and crew training period. She wore this Ms. 12R camouflage pattern for only a short time, until she put to sea to work with the British Royal Navy.

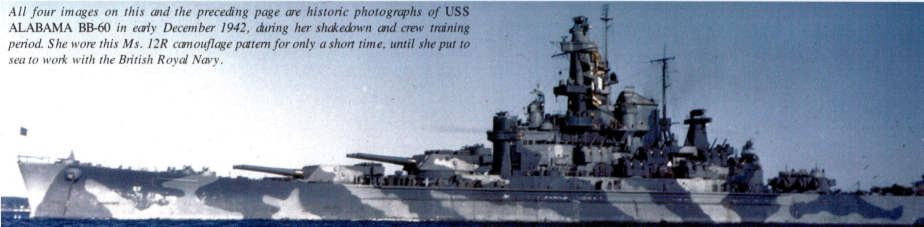

Looking over the aft deck of SOUTH DAKOTA *as she steams out of* Scapa Flow, *with her sistership* ALABAMA *following astern, in her wake, who was also being followed by* HMS ANSON, *visible just beyond* HMS SHEFFIELD. *The capital warship beyond her was* HMS RENOWN. *Both of these RN warships just completed major refits and were freshly painted at the time of this photo, which puts the date about mid to late July 1943.*

The small inset image is of one of BB-57's OS2U Kingfisher *observation aircraft being loaded onto the ship's catapult, during June 1943, in Scapa Flow.*

This image was taken from the bridge of the SOUTH DAKOTA *while she was operating with the RN battleship* HMS DUKE OF YORK *and the aircraft carrier* HMS UNI-CORN. *They sortied off the Norwegian coast, near Sognefiord, 23 July 1943, in an attempt to lure out the German battleships* TIRPITZ *and* SCHARNHORST.

Both this and the photograph on the following page were taken aboard SOUTH DAKOTA during 1944. In this image her band is practicing aft of turret #3, which is trained to starboard. The rest of the crewmembers in this image are relaxing in the hot summer sun of the Pacific Ocean. The image on the following page is of BB-57's OS2Us undergoing some maintenance time.

USS INDIANA *at sea in August 1943, operating in the Solomon Island theater.*

USS ALABAMA, *Hampton Roads, 20 August 1943, just out of the Norfolk Navy Yard at the conclusion of a refit and overhaul.*

Both of the images on this page are of the USS ALABAMA, 20 August 1943. She was painted into a Ms. 21 camouflage, which was an overall painting of Navy Blue on all vertical surfaces and Deck Blue on all decks and horizontal surfaces.

This contemporary photograph of the MASSACHUSETTS shows how much of her WWII configuration she retained. This image was taken 30 May 1987.

This contemporary photograph of the ALABAMA, like the image to the left, shows how much of her WWII configuration she retained. This image was taken 1 January 1980.

Another photograph of ALABAMA *at the conclusion of her refit at the Norfolk Navy Yard, taken 20 August 1943. Navy personnel have marked the image with the upgrades that were made to the battleship during that refit. Adjacent to the waist Mk. 37 director tower, a Mk. 51 AA director and tub was installed, as well as modifications to the foremast. Not marked, but fitted, was an additional SG radar antenna atop the mainmast, then giving BB-60 a radar sweep of 360°, whereas she only had 270° previously. Interestingly enough, she did not receive an upgrade to her air search radar, the older SC antenna visible atop her foremast.*

USS SOUTH DAKOTA BB-57 *departing the Norfolk Navy Yard, 20 August 1943, at the conclusion of a minor refit after her service with the Royal Navy's Home Fleet. She retained her Ms. 21 camouflage configuration with a fresh application. The one thing that was unique about BB-57 was the quad 40mm mount at the bow. Because she had a reduced 5in. battery, she was able to mount a larger 40mm AA battery.*

Some of the additions made to BB-57 at this refit were circled in these photographs. Like BB-60, SOUTH DAKOTA also received a Mk. 51 AA director and tub, both port and starboard, amidships. She also received an electronics upgrade to her Mk. 8 FC radar atop the Mk. 38 foretop main battery director. The largest upgrade to BB-57 was the addition of the SK air search radar system, the antenna mounted atop the foremast. This SK system was much stronger and more accurate than the previous SC system.

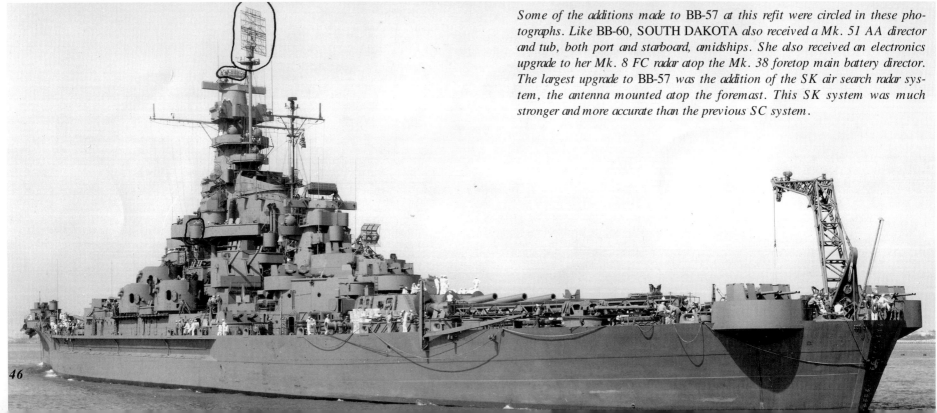

INDIANA and MASSACHUSETTS continued their support role in the Guadalcanal area, based out of Noumea, New Caledonia. By 17 May 1943, the British Royal Navy aircraft carrier HMS VICTORIOUS arrived as a replacement to ENTERPRISE, which needed an overhaul. VICTORIOUS, outfitted with USN aircraft and additional AA mounts, operated with SARATOGA, protected by the battleships NORTH CAROLINA, MASSACHUSETTS and INDIANA. For the rest of May, and into June, this group, with cruisers and destroyers trained in the seas near New Caledonia. The same training for the aircraft carriers, supported by the three fast battleships, continued through July, in an effort to cross train USN and RN aviators, while protecting USN warships in the Solomon Island area. While training, this TF also supported the operations in the New Georgia campaign.

By the beginning of August 1943, INDIANA was en route to Pearl Harbor to re-supply, arriving there on 9 August. By the end of August, BB-58 departed with the new aircraft carriers USS ESSEX CV-9, YORKTOWN CV-10 and INDEPENDENCE CVL-22, cruisers and destroyers on a surprise raid upon the Japanese stronghold at Marcus Island. This raid took place on 1 September 1943, with complete success, decimating the Japanese there. This completed, INDIANA returned to Pearl Harbor for a refit.

In the meantime SOUTH DAKOTA and ALABAMA departed the Norfolk Navy Yard, 21 August 1943, bound for the Pacific theater of operations. They transited the Panama Canal, stopped at Pearl Harbor, arriving at Havannah Harbor, Efate Island, in the New Hebrides chain of islands, 14 September 1943. They trained with the new ESSEX class aircraft carriers for the remainder of September and all of October 1943. The summer of 1943 was a time of recuperation for the US Navy, due to the heavy losses they incurred with the fighting during the Guadalcanal campaign. This was also a time that the US Navy designed and refined new tactics and much training was need for this. By early November, US Naval forces re-grouped in the Fiji Islands to start the new campaign of "Island Hopping" towards victory over Japan.

USS INDIANA BB-58 underway in the Pacific Ocean, 24 January 1944. She was painted in a Measure 32 - Pattern 11D (Ms. 32/11D), also known as a "Dazzle Pattern" camouflage. The paint colors for this camouflage consisted of Light Gray (5-L), Ocean Gray (5-O) and Dull Black (BK) on vertical surfaces and 5-O and Deck Blue (20-B) on decks and horizontal surfaces.

INDIANA *steaming with Task Force 58.1 on 27 January 1944, en route to attack Taroa Island airfield, Maloelap Atoll, Marshall Islands, wearing a Ms. 32/11D camouflage, the only* SOUTH DAKOTA *class battleship to wear a dazzle camouflage. Taken by a* USS ENTERPRISE CV-6 *photographer.*

USS SOUTH DAKOTA BB-57, *29 January 1944. She was screening the carriers of* TF-58 *during the attack upon the Marshall Islands. This photograph, taken on the above date, is off of the Kwajalein Atoll, shot from the fleet carrier* USS INTREPID CV-11, *with the battleship* NORTH CAROLINA, *the light carrier* MONTEREY CVL-26 *and the heavy cruiser* INDIANAPOLIS CA-35 *in background.*

Another view of BB-57 from an aircraft from USS BUNKER HILL CV-17, *dated 24 January 1944, en route to the large scale attack upon the Japanese forces entrenched throughout the Marshall Islands. BB-60 is in the background, as the two battleships were en route to bombard the islands of Roi and Namur, 1 February 1944.*

The next offensive involving the SOUTH DAKOTA class battleships against the Japanese began with the attack and liberation of the vast Gilbert and Marshall Islands, starting in November 1943. ALABAMA was part of the screen for the carrier YORKTOWN in the invasion of Tarawa. When that operation was secured, she joined her sistership SOUTH DAKOTA and WASHINGTON to screen the TG around BUNKER HILL and her TF. They would then steam to bombard the island of Nauru, after which, they escorted the carriers back to the New Hebrides, then onto Pearl Harbor, arriving 12 January 1944, with the SOUTH DAKOTA remaining at Efate, New Hebrides.

INDIANA and MASSACHUSETTS were the screen for the ENTERPRISE carrier TG on those raids upon Tarawa, in the Gilberts, and other island airfields, as well as their bombardment and that upon Nauru. Both battleships moved on to bombard Kwajalein and it's airfield in late January 1944.

BB-59 en route to attack Taroa Island airfield on the Maloelap Atoll, in the Marshall Islands, taken from CV-6 aircraft, 27 January 1944.

20mm gun crews aboard BB-58.

53

INDIANA *being eased into a dry dock at the Pearl Harbor Navy Yard, after her arrival there 14 February 1944.* *Note the missing rangefinder, catapult and after 40mm AA mount, as well as the extensive damage to her hull.*

Another view of INDIANA *in a dry dock at the Pearl Harbor Navy Yard, after her arrival there 14 February 1944.*

This is another image of the battleship SOUTH DAKOTA at sea during the assault upon the Marshall Islands, taken from an aircraft from BUNKER HILL, 24 January 1944.

BB-57 at anchor in the harbor at Majuro Island, the Marshall Islands, 8 April 1944. There is a BALTIMORE class heavy cruiser beyond her stern and the USS WICHITA CA-45 is at anchor beyond her bow.

MASSACHUSETTS *slowing moving forward, just out of the Puget Sound Naval Shipyard, 11 July 1944. She finely received a major upgrade to her air search radar with the addition of the SK system, the antenna mounted on the foremast. She also had her SG surface search radar upgraded by mounting the antenna atop both the fore and aft masts.*

During this refit BB-59 also received a pair of 40mm quad AA mounts on the foredeck.

In the pre-dawn hours of 1 February 1944, INDIANA was in a serious collision with WASHINGTON, disabling both warships. While maneuvering to refuel, BB-58 turned in front of BB-56, unable to avoid INDIANA, crushed almost 100ft. of her bow, severely holing BB-58 on her starboard side. BB-56's fore deck ripped the rangefinder off turret #3, slid along INDIANA's deck, also ripping off the catapult and starboard aft 40mm mount, before collapsing onto her crushed bow. The crippled battleships limped to Majuro for temporary repairs before steaming for Pearl Harbor.

MASSACHUSETTS, SOUTH DAKO- TA and ALABAMA, still screening carrier TFs, took part in the mid-February raid upon the primary IJN forward anchorage at Truk with devastating results to the Japanese Navy. The three sisterships would continue their carrier screen duties during the raids upon the Marianas, with strikes upon Tinian, Saipan and Guam. During this operation, a 5in. mount aboard ALABAMA accidentally fired into another 5in. mount killing 5 crewmen, 21 February 1944. They returned to Majuro by the end of February 1944.

The three SOUTH DAKOTA class battleships later sortied for carrier strike operations with TF-58 against strongholds in the Caroline Islands at Palau, Yap, Ulithi, and Woleai, 22 March 1944. The battleships returned briefly to Majuro to re-supply and then departed to cover carrier strikes against various airfield targets and cover US troop landings along the New Guinea coast.

INDIANA, just returned from Pearl Harbor, collision damage repaired, joined her three sisterships and was able to participate in a second strike upon the IJN base at Truk, 29-30 April 1944. Afterwards, MASSACHUSETTS departed for Puget Sound Naval Shipyard for a major refit, while the other three returned to Majuro to re-supply.

USS SOUTH DAKOTA *at sea, August 1944. She is just steaming out of the Puget Sound Naval Shipyard 21 August 1944.*

MASSACHUSETTS *during an underway replenishment (UNREP) with the fleet tanker USS KASKASKIA AO-27, 17 October 1944.*

USS INDIANA BB-58 *out of Puget Sound Naval Shipyard, 30 November 1944. She was then painted in a Ms. 22 camouflage.*

MASSACHUSETTS arrived at the Puget Sound for a major refit to re-line her main and secondary gun barrels. She completed this task on 11 July 1944. She arrived at Pearl Harbor, departing there on 1 August for Eniwetok, the Marshall Islands. BB-59 later departed 30 August for the Philippine Islands.

SOUTH DAKOTA, INDIANA and ALABAMA spent a month, beginning 4 May, exercising and performing minor refits at Majuro, Marshall Islands. This was to prepare for the invasion of the Mariana Islands. Departing Majuro, 5 June 1944, as part of TF-58, the three sisterships screened carrier strike

groups and performed bombardment duties as they assaulted the Marianas.

On 13 June 1944, BB-57, 58 and 60 with four other battleships, bombarded Saipan and Tinian with both their main and secondary batteries. Back to guarding the fast carrier strike groups, SOUTH DAKOTA was hit by a 500lb.

bomb on her main deck, 19 June. Damage was heavy, with 24 killed and as many wounded. BB-57 managed to continue fighting during what would become known as the "Battle of the Philippine Sea." ALABAMA was near-missed, but INDIANA narrowly escaped a torpedo only to be hit in the hull side by a crashing Japanese aircraft. Debris scattered over her deck, but caused little damage. The IJN losses were huge, with over 300 aircraft shot down by USN aircraft and warships and they lost two fleet carriers. The US Navy carrier strike forces continued their conquest of the Marianas, with the primary focus on Guam through to the end of June 1944.

SOUTH DAKOTA departed Ulithi 27 June for Puget Sound for an overhaul and refit,

arriving there 10 July. Her overhaul was short, departing 26 August for Pearl Harbor, then back to Ulithi to join TF-38 and screen the fast carrier strike groups.

MASSACHUSETTS trained with carriers in preparation for the pending invasion of the Philippine Islands during the month of September. She was an AA escort for the carrier strike groups because of her powerful AA armament, as were the other fast battleships. Their speed was also another reason these battleships were used extensively with the fast carrier strike groups.

ALABAMA and INDIANA continued to steam in the area around the Marianas to protect US landing forces on Saipan, screening the fast carrier strike groups as they struck enemy

shipping, airfields, and shore installations on Guam, Tinian and Saipan. They later returned to the Marshall Islands for maintenance by early July. During the remainder of July and into August, BB-60 continued to support the fast carrier strike groups as AA escort, and to protect landings on Guam, Palau, Ulithi, and Yap. During September they continued their support of the fast carrier strike groups in the preparation of the coming invasion of Leyte, the Philippines.

INDIANA departed in early October for a much need refit and overhaul. She was bound for Puget Sound, arriving at that Navy Yard, 23 October 1944. She would be there for more than a month of round the clock work and not depart for Pearl Harbor until 6 December 1944.

USS MASSACHUSETTS BB-59 *at sea in UNREP with the fleet oiler* USS SAUGATUCK AO 75, *en route to bombard Japan. This photograph was taken from the fleet aircraft carrier* USS HORNET CV-12, 20 April 1945.

USS ALABAMA BB-60, *12 March 1945, departing the Puget Sound Naval Shipyard after a minor refit and overhaul. This was mostly routine, but she did suffer some damage from the massive typhoon encountered in mid-December 1944. One of the upgrades during this refit was the addition of SK-2 radar, the antenna on her foremast. Another addition was the then new SR air search radar system, a redundant system to SK, or SK-2, it's antenna installed on the mainmast.*

The image to the right is a great view of many of the fitted antenna during this refit in February 1945. Note that BB-60 also received an upgrade to her main battery fire control radar, with the then new Mk. 13 FC antenna fitted atop the forward main battery director.

SOUTH DAKOTA *in a floating dry dock at Guam,*
sometime during May 1945.

SOUTH DAKOTA joined TF-38 with MASSACHUSETTS and ALABAMA and sortied 6 October 1944 for air attacks upon Okinawa. In mid-October they supported carrier strikes against shipping and shore installations on Formosa.

The three SOUTH DAKOTA class battleships were screening a fast carrier strike force of TF-38 when the landings on Leyte took place on 20 October 1944. The largest naval battle in history began on 22 October 1944, known as the "Battle of Leyte Gulf," was so large that it was broken down into several battles over a six day period. The battleships and their flock of fast carriers steamed north towards a Japanese force deliberately set up as a decoy. The American fleet fell for the ruse. The Japanese plan almost worked, had it not been for the damage previously inflicted upon them in the early stages of the battle. The IJN just could not press forward their attack successfully. They had gambled everything and by the end of this battle, their losses were substantial. They were never again able to assemble an effective striking force.

The fast carrier strike force that the three SOUTH DAKOTA class battleships were supporting did strike the IJN diversionary force with a vengeance, sinking four IJN carriers, a cruiser and a destroyer. This was known as the "Battle off Cape Engano," one of the lesser battles of the "Battle of Leyte Gulf." Due to this circumstance, the fast battleships were not able to engage the IJN battleships, as they so badly wanted to.

After the retreat of the Imperial Japanese Navy out of the Philippine Islands, the US Navy continued with air strikes against air fields and shore installations on many of the Philippine Islands, including Luzon, Manila and Mindoro throughout the month of November. SOUTH DAKOTA, MASSACHUSETTS and ALABAMA continued to support this force. They returned to Ulithi on 24 November 1944, the three battleships re-supplied and their crew's rested for 16 days.

In the meantime, INDIANA arrived at Pearl Harbor on 12 December. She conducted training exercises with other fleet units for nine days in Hawaiian waters. BB-58 departed for bombardment duty in the invasion of Iwo Jima, 10 January 1945, via Eniwetok and Saipan. Bombardment of Iwo Jima took place on 24 January with little resistance. She departed Iwo Jima for Ulithi, arriving there 26 January for two weeks of re-supplying and crew rest.

A view aboard INDIANA, taken from the aft deck, sometime in early 1945. The radar antenna atop the mainmast is for her SM, or SP fighter control radar system. The two antenna were very similar to each other, but the two performed the same functions. SPs were fitted to battleships and cruisers more frequently. This was a height finding radar that was very accurate.

INDIANA *and* MASSACHUSETTS *at sea off the coast of Japan, 14 July 1945. They were conducting a bombardment of the Imperial Ironworks at Kamaishi, on the island of Honshu. The heavy cruisers in the background of this image were* QUINCY *and* CHICAGO.

SOUTH DAKOTA, MASSACHU-SETTS and ALABAMA departed Ulithi 10 December 1944 in support of fast carrier strike groups in air assaults upon Japanese forces on Luzon. These started on 14 December with attacks upon air fields in an effort to neutralize Japanese retaliation for the US invasion upon Mindoro. The mission was completed by 17 December and as the fleet attempted to refuel at sea, UNREP, they were surprised by a massive typhoon. Rough seas and very high winds made refueling impossible by the 18th. Winds reached speeds of 120 knots, with seas as high as 40 to 50ft. When the storm cleared the area by 20 December, the US Navy lost three destroyers, severe damage to a cruiser and several carriers, with many warships receiving minor storm damage. Of the three SOUTH DAKOTA class battleships, ALABAMA received the most damage, losing all of her OS2U Kingfisher aircraft in the largest storm the US Navy had ever weathered. The three battleships retired with the Third Fleet to Ulithi on 24 December, making repairs and re-supplying. ALABAMA departed for Puget Sound Naval Shipyard, 26 December 1944.

SOUTH DAKOTA and MASSACHU-SETTS supported the fast carrier strike groups in their assaults from 30 December through 26 January 1945. They made air strikes upon Formosa, Luzon, Camranh Bay, Hong Kong and Okinawa. The Third Fleet returned to Ulithi to re-supply on 28 January. INDIANA had just arrived at Ulithi two days earlier.

The Fifth Fleet sortied from Ulithi on 10 February 1945, the three SOUTH DAKOTA class battleships BB-57, 58 and 59, included, for waters off of Iwo Jima and Japan for operations for the invasion of Iwo Jima.

SOUTH DAKOTA *at sea, 21 August 1945, off of Japan, as part of the fleet kept in reserve off of Japan in case of a surprise attack during the time of Japan's surrender.*

(BB59)

MASSACHUSETTS *at the conclusion of a refit at the Puget Sound Naval Shipyard, 22 January 1946. Note that the wood decks are no longer painted and warship was painted in a Ms. 22 camouflage. There was also a large reduction of 20mm single AA mounts at that time.*

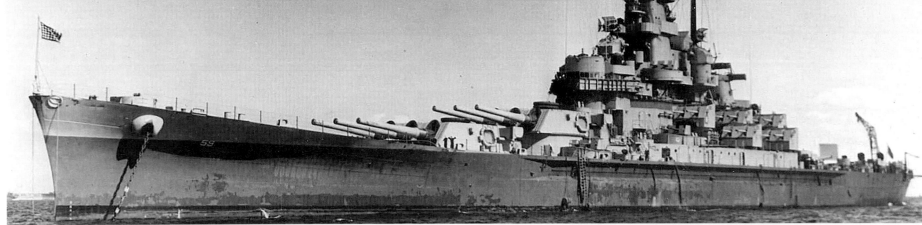

USS MASSACHUSETTS BB-59 *at the conclusion of her final refit in January 1946, at the Puget Sound Naval Shipyard. She was repainted again with the Ms. 22 camouflage pattern, but due to the shortage of blue pigment at that time, there was a chance that she was painted with neutral grays. Note the SR radar antenna on her mainmast.*

The invasion of Iwo Jima began on 16 February 1945 with air strikes on that island. BB-57, 58 and 59 all supported the fast carrier strike groups in this operation, first of the Japanese home island of Honshu in an effort to disable Japanese land based air power. By 17 February, they moved to launch strikes upon Iwo Jima. The next day the three fast battle- ships bombarded Iwo Jima with their 16in. guns. They stayed in the vicinity of Iwo Jima until they guarded the carriers on strikes upon Tokyo on 25 February and then Okinawa on 1 March 1945. TF-58 arrived back at Ulithi on 3 March to re-supply.

Task Force 58 departed Ulithi 14 March 1945 with the SOUTH DAKOTA, INDIANA and MASSACHUSETTS as support for the fast carrier strike groups to operate air strikes against Japan to disable Japanese air power and any remaining naval strength. The air strikes were against the IJN bases and IJA air fields at Kobe, Kure and Kyushu on 18 and 19 March. While guarding the fast carriers, the three SOUTH DAKOTA class battleships and other

USS INDIANA BB-58 *at sea, just out of her final refit at the Puget Sound Naval Shipyard in February 1946. She is also painted in Ms. 22. Note the reduction of 20mm AA mounts.*

escorts present were unable to stop some of the hundreds of kamikazes, one striking the carrier USS FRANKLIN CV-17, 19 March. She was badly damaged and by a miracle was saved by her crew and able to limp home to the USA.

TF-58 then moved to launch air strikes upon Okinawa on 23 March. The next day the battleships bombarded southeastern Okinawa. TF-58 again struck air fields on Kyushu on 29 March. They returned to Okinawa and pounded targets there from 31 March through 3 April 1945, during the invasion.

On 7 April, the fast carrier strike groups launched an attack upon the IJN's super battleship YAMATO, as she was attempting to reach Okinawa and the USN invasion fleet. She was sunk with air strikes, a big disappointment to the crews of USN battleships that all wanted a chance to slug it out with any of the IJN battleships.

On 11 April, more kamikazes started to break through the carrier screen and crash into the HANCOCK CV-19, badly damaging her and putting her out of action. The three BB-57 type battleships present continued to guard the remaining carriers in operations against Okinawa and the Japanese homeland into May 1945. They returned to Ulithi to re-supply at that time.

On 6 May 1945, SOUTH DAKOTA had an accident in the turret #2 magazine with a flash fire from the dropping of powder charges that necessitated the flooding of that magazine. Eleven crew were killed with 24 wounded. The ship was lucky that the magazine was flooded as quickly as it was, as the magazine could have

exploded and sunk the battleship. BB-57 was able to make for Guam on her own power, where she was dry docked and repaired until 1 July 1945.

In the meantime, ALABAMA, back from her refit at Puget Sound, joined the TF-58, departing Ulithi 9 May 1945, bound for fast carrier strikes upon Kyushu, Japan. She was joined in her screening role by INDIANA and MASSACHUSETTS. While operating off of Japan, TF-58 was hit by many kamikazes, some getting through. Carriers were the primary target, with INTREPID CV-11, BUNKER HILL CV-17 and ENTERPRISE CV-6, all badly damaged and out of action.

On 5 June 1945, TF-58 was hit by another typhoon. Wind speeds of 140 knots were measured, with seas as high as 50ft. Two cruisers were damaged and a carrier lost her forward flight deck. Many ships received heavy storm damage. INDIANA lost steering for 35 minutes, also losing power from one engine, lost one OS2U and was nearly swamped. She managed to regain power and steering and headed for the Philippines to repair damages.

All four SOUTH DAKOTA class battleships joined TG-38 for attacks upon the Japanese home islands with both air strikes and bombardments. They departed Leyte Gulf 1 July 1945 and headed for Japan. Initially they guarded carriers on their air strikes upon Tokyo, then three of the class BB-57, 58 and 59 bombarded the Imperial Ironworks at Kamaishi, Honshu, 14 July. Later on the night of 17-18 July, all four SOUTH DAKOTA class battleships bombarded six major industrial plants on

Honshu, eight miles from Tokyo.

The four battleships of the SOUTH DAKOTA continued to support the fast carrier strike groups for the remainder of July with strikes on industrial centers and military installations on Honshu and Hokkaido. The battleships bombarded Honshu again on 29 July, and once more on 9 August 1945. There was one last group of carrier strikes on 13 and 15 August before Japan capitulated late in the day on 15 August. SOUTH DAKOTA and INDIANA were present in Tokyo Bay for the surrender signing aboard the USS MISSOURI BB-63 on 2 September 1945. MASSACHUSETTS headed back to Puget Sound on 1 September for a refit and ALABAMA screened carriers off of Japan, but later entered Tokyo Bay on 5 September.

All four of the SOUTH DAKOTA class battleships performed "Magic Carpet Duty," transporting US service personnel back to the USA during the months after the surrender of Japan. They then all received minor refits postwar and were put into the reserve fleet. BB-57 was decommissioned on 31 January 1947, BB-58 on 11 September 1947, BB-59 on 27 March 1947, and BB-60 on 9 January 1947, all in the Reserve Fleet. Then, much later BB-57 was sold for scrapping on 25 October 1962 and BB-58 on 6 September 1963. BB-59 and BB-60 were both saved for memorial status, with MASSACHUSETTS going to Fall River, Massachusetts in 1965 and ALABAMA going to Mobile, Alabama in 1964. Both battleships still exist as memorials as of the date of this book's printing.

ALABAMA *at Mobile, Alabama as a museum. This photo was taken in January 1980. She and the MASS-ACHUSETTS* largely retained their configuration from their last refit.

GENERAL STATISTICS

Dimensions (ft.)

length overall...680.00
beam...108.20
draught   (min.).........................29.50
                 (max.).......................36.50

Displacement (tons)

as built light.......................................35,412
          standard..................................37,970
          full load...............................44,519
1945   full load.............................45,231

Armor (in.)

main belt..12.25 to 7.25
decks...5.3 to 5.0
turrets...................16 face, 7 roof, 12 sides, 10 rear
bulkheads...13.4
barbettes...17.3 to 11.5
conning tower...................................15 + 7.25 roof

Propulsion

boilers   8........................Babcock & Willcox
engines   4......General Electric geared turbines
speed
(1941)..27.00kts

(1945)..26.80kts
shaft horsepower (forward)............................133,000
                  (astern)................................32,000
fuel capacity (normal)...............................6,673 tons
fuel capacity (max)...................................7,127 tons

Endurance

18,500nm @ 10kts   15,020nm @ 15kts
10,610nm @ 20kts   5,950nm @ 25kts

Aircraft

1941-1946.............................2 or 3x Vought OS2U-3
1945-1947.................................1 or 3x Curtiss SC-1

Complement

1942....................145 officers...................2,112 men
1945....................168 officers...................2,500 men

Armament Summary

as designed or fitted

Main Battery
9x 16in./45cal.(406mm)(three gun turrets)
Secondary Battery (dual purpose)
20x 5in./38cal.(127mm)(two gun turrets)
Note: BB-57 fitted with *16x* 5in./38cal.
Medium Anti-Aircraft
4x 1.1in.(quad AA mounts)
Light Anti-Aircraft
12x 20mm(single AA mounts)
Anti-Aircraft Weapon Changes (WWII)
BB-57

.50cal

03/42	*1.1in Quad Mount*	
	03/42	09/42
8	7	5

20mm

03/42	09/42	02/43	12/44	03/45
16	36+	35	72	77

40mm Quad Mount

09/42	02/43	12/44	03/45
4	17	18	17

BB-58

20mm

06/42	11/42	10/43	12/44
16	35	56	56

40mm Quad Mount

06/42	11/42	10/43	12/44
6	6	12	12

BB-59

20mm

04/42	11/42	01/43	02/43	06/44	09/44
12	35	50	61	52	38

40mm Quad Mount

04/42	11/42	01/43	02/43	06/44	09/44
6	6	10	12	16	18

BB-60

20mm

04/42	01/43	03/43	04/43	02/45
12	35	40	52	56

40mm Quad Mount

04/42	01/43	03/43	04/43	02/45
6	8	12	12	12

Directors

Main Battery	Mk. 38
Secondary Battery	Mk. 37
40mm Battery	Mk. 51 & Mk. 57

Fire Control Radar

	1942	1943	1945
Main Batt.	Mk. 3	Mk. 8	Mk. 13
Secondary Batt.	Mk. 4		Mk. 12/22
40mm Batt.	Mk. 51		Mk. 51 & 57

Search Radar

	1942	1944	1945
Air Search	SC	SK	SK-2
Surface Search	SG		SG & SU

Cost to Build

BB-59   May 1942 $76,885,750.00

REFERENCES

Action in the Pacific
L. Sowinski, Naval Institute Press, 1981
Naval Radar
N. Friedman, Conway Maritime Press, 1988
Naval Weapons of WWII
J. Campbell, Conway Maritime Press, 1985
Ship's Data USS Massachusetts BB-59
A.S. Lott, R. F. Sumrall, Leeward Publications, 1973
Ship's Data 2: USS Alabama BB-60
A.S. Lott, R. F. Sumrall, Leeward Publications, 1974
Ships & Aircraft of the U. S. Fleet
J. C. Fahey, Ships & Aircraft Press, 1945
U. S. Battleships
N. Friedman, Naval Institute Press, 1985
U. S. Battleships, 1935-1992
W. Garzke & R. Dulin, Naval Institute Press, 1976
U. S. Naval Weapons
N. Friedman, Naval Institute Press, 1985
USS Massachusetts: Technical Reference 2
R. S. Shoker, Oxford Museum Press, 2004

RESOURCES

The Floating Dry dock
P. O. Box 9587, Treasure Island, FL 33740
Web Site: www.floatingdrydock.com
U. S. Naval Historical Center
805 Kidder Breese SE, Bldg # 57
Washington Navy Yard, Washington DC, 20374-5060
Still Photos (202)433-2765 • Web Site: www.history.navy.mil
U. S. National Archives @ College Park
8601 Adelphi Rd., College Park, MD. 20740-6001
(301)713-6800 • Web Site: www.nara.gov

ACKNOWLEDGMENTS

Classic Warships
would like to express it's gratitude for assistance from the following individuals -

**Ron Smith • Randy Shoker
Pete Clayton • Don Montgomery
Don Preul**

WARSHIP PICTORIAL SERIES

at the time of this printing

USS YORKTOWN CV-10, *the subject of the next book in the Warship Pictorial series.*

Front Cover:
USS ALABAMA BB-60 *during her shakedown cruise in the north Atlantic Ocean, off the coast of Maine, December 1942.*

Back Cover:
Top Photo: BB-60 *at anchor in Lynn Haven Roads during December 1942.*
Bottom Photo: USS INDIANA BB-58 *firing upon the Kamaishi Steel Works factory on the Japanese main island of Honshu.*